Cute Pets

You rock

You are the heart and the soul

Authors / Images and Cover

Dirk L. Feiler

Tanja Feiler

The outfits

The girls working hard for making the second edition of outfits for the concerts of the Cute Pets.

The others working on the studio.

Special mails

Kittys Family, Mr. And Mrs. Feiler getting mails by the president and the first lady. Kitty looking in her mails a special mail, which she gets

by Mrs. Feiler.
Some Mails have
Kitty, and this
are the special
mails by Barack
Obama   and
Michelle.

Organizing for Action <info@barackobama.com> schrieb am 17:27 Donnerstag, 26.September 2013:

Friend --

The First Lady knows exactly how important the grassroots work we're doing is.

If you haven't responded to her

question yet, take a minute -- answer this one-question survey and let us know what gets you fired up:

http://my.barack obama.com/Just-One-Question

Thanks,

Organizing for Action

Original Message----------

-

From: Michelle Obama

Subject: Hey, it's me

Friend --

You can't just want change.

You've got to fight for it, too. Barack and

I hear that's exactly what you're doing -- thank you.

This work matters. Just look at the August congressional recess: For the first time in a long time, our side built some real momentum over the summer -- on everything from immigration reform to climate change. That's all you.

You're the heart and soul

of this organization. That's why OFA wants to hear directly from you.

So, if you had to pick, what is the number one issue that

drives you to keep fighting?

http://my.barack obama.com/Just-One-Question

I had the privilege of helping get Organizing for

Action off the
ground earlier
this year, and
I'm excited
about where
you're taking
it.

There's a lot
of work still
ahead. As Barack
says: Winning an

election doesn't bring about the change we seek. It simply gives us the chance to make that change.

You're embracing that opportunity -- and all

Americans will be better off for it.

Thanks,

Michelle

This email was sent to:

> info@feiler-
verlag.org.

The newspaper

Haeschen making an report about the project Daycare and now the newspaper knocking on the door of Cute Pets

The newspaper making a interview and written an articel, next day publishing on the newspaper. A friend of Cute Pets, which visiting the band, read out:

You rock

The Cute Pets are famous here in Petcity.

Musicians , authors and artists, designers , this is the Urbanization . Meanwhile, two members are married to members of Urbanization . They provide with its diverse art for the advancement of Petcity . Your latest song is daycare on the social project . We all look forward to the new album and concerts . The new album is

almost   finished
.   New   concert
tour ?

www.ingramcontent.com/pod-product-compliance
Lightning Source LLC
Chambersburg PA
CBHW050927290526
45792CB00002B/916